Salah

The Guide Book for Prayer

CONTENTS

FOREWORD

This booklet is a guide book to teach Muslims how to perform prayer. The way of performing prayer has been described in simple language and with illustrations. Its essential and recommended acts are outlined and its basic requirements are detailed. All the information is based on authentic traditions of the Prophet (peace and blessing of Allāh be upon him) who commanded his followers to perform prayer as they saw him doing. The difference of opinions among the Muslim scholars has been shown. In some cases more than one supplications are given for a particular act; the reader has the option to choose what he likes, or if he so wishes, he can read them all. However, it is always rewarding to choose what has been reported from the Prophet (peace and blessing of Allāh be upon him) through authentic sources.

May Allāh guide us to the way of His Prophet Muhammad (peace and blessing of Allāh be upon him) and keep us away from going astray and following vain desires. May the Almighty accept our prayers and grant us good rewards for them.

INTRODUCTION

Prayer is the most important pillar of Islam. Indeed it is the dividing line between Islam and infidelity. It is a duty incumbent on every Muslim, male or female, who has attained the age of maturity and has a sound mind. There are numerous verses in the Holy Qur'ān commanding Muslims to observe prayers regularly. The Almighty Allāh says:

حَافِظُوا عَلَى الصَّلَوَاتِ وَ الصَّلٰوةِ الْوُسْطٰى

"Guard the prayers strictly, especially the middle prayer (i.e., 'Asr)." (2/238)

اِنَّ الصَّلٰوةَ كَانَتْ عَلَى الْمُؤْمِنِينَ كِتٰبًا مَّوْقُوتًا ۝

"Verily, the prayer is enjoined on the believers at stated times." (4/103)

The Messenger of Allāh (peace and blessing of Allāh be upon him) constantly reminded the community, of the importance of prayer and warned them of the consequences of neglecting it.

Abdullah bin Mas'ud (may Allāh bless him) narrated:

I asked the Messenger of Allāh (peace and blessing of Allāh be upon him): "Which of the actions is the best?"

He replied: "Prayer at its stated time." I said: "What comes next?" He replied: "Kindness to parents." I further asked: "What comes next?" He replied: "Struggle in the cause of Allāh." *(Bukhāri and Muslim)*

In another *Hadith,* the Prophet (peace and blessing of Allāh be upon him) asked his Companions:

"Tell me, if one of you had a river at his door and took bath in it five times a day, would there remain any dirt on his body?" The Companions replied: "No, no dirt would be left on his body." The Prophet (peace and blessing of Allāh be upon him) said: "This is the example of the five prayers by which Allāh washes away the sins."
(Bukhāri and Muslim)

The Prophet (peace and blessing of Allāh be upon him) said in yet another *Hadith:*

"The dividing line between a believer and the disbeliever is the negligence of prayer." *(Muslim)*

In another report the Messenger of Allāh (peace and blessing of Allāh be upon him) said:

"The first thing about which a person will be asked on the Day of Judgement will be the prayer."
(Abu Dāwud and At-Tirmidhi)

PREPARATION
for PRAYER

When one intends to perform prayer, one has to make sure that the following conditions are fulfilled:

1. The first condition is cleanliness. This includes the cleanliness of the body, the dress and the place where the prayer is to be performed.

2. Second is the covering of the private parts of the body. This means, in the case of a man, to cover the parts of the body from the navel down to the knees. Shoulders must also be covered - because the Messenger of Allāh (peace and blessing of Allāh be upon him) said:

"None of you should observe prayer in a single garment which does not cover his shoulders." *(Bukhāri and Muslim)* A woman is required to cover all of her body except the hands and the face.

3. Third is the commencement of the stated time. Prayer performed before the stated time is not valid. The stated time for each of the five daily prayers is as follows:

i) The time for *Fajr* (morning) prayer is between the break of dawn and sunrise.

ii) The time of *Zuhr* (noon) prayer starts when the sun declines from the meridian, and ends when the shadow of an object becomes equal to it in length.

iii) The time of *'Asr* (afternoon) prayer begins when the time of *Zuhr* ends, and lasts until sunset.

iv) The time of *Maghrib* (sunset) prayer starts with the sunset, and ends with the disappearance of the red line from the horizon.

v) The time of *'Isha'* (night) prayer begins when the time of *Maghrib* ends, and remains until the *Fajr*.

4. Facing the direction of the Ka'bah in Makkah is the fourth condition for the validity of the prayer.

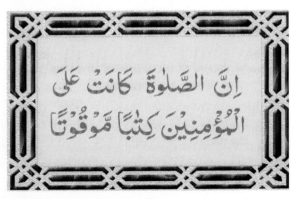

Prayer is enjoined on believers at stated times

Cleanliness

Cleanliness is of two types:

i) *Ghusl* or washing of the whole body;

ii) *Wudu'* or ritual ablution.

Both are required for the validity of the prayer. The first, i.e. *Ghusl* becomes compulsory in the following cases:

i) after sexual intercourse;

ii) after ejaculation of semen by any reason;

iii) when the monthly menstruation of a woman has ended;

iv) when a woman's postnatal bleeding stops;

v) and when a non-Muslim embraces Islam.

Ghusl is performed by washing the private parts and removing the filth from the body, then performing the ritual ablution without washing the feet, then washing the whole body. The feet should be washed at the end.

Wudu' or Ritual Ablution

Ablution is a requisite for prayer. Allāh, the Exalted said:

يَٰٓأَيُّهَا الَّذِينَ ءَامَنُوٓا إِذَا قُمْتُمْ إِلَى الصَّلَوٰةِ فَٱغْسِلُوا۟ وُجُوهَكُمْ وَأَيْدِيَكُمْ إِلَى الْمَرَافِقِ وَٱمْسَحُوا۟ بِرُءُوسِكُمْ وَأَرْجُلَكُمْ إِلَى الْكَعْبَيْنِ ط

"O you who believe! When you rise up for prayer,
wash your faces and your hands up to the elbows, and
lightly rub your heads (with wet hands) and (wash)
your feet up to the ankles." (5/6)

The Prophet (peace and blessing of Allāh be upon him)
said:

"Allāh does not accept prayer without ablution."

How to perform Ablution

1. Make the intention in your mind to make ablution. There is no need to express your intention in words.

2. Say Bismillāh (In the Name of Allāh).

3. Wash the hands up to the wrists.

4. Rinse the mouth. Clean your teeth with a *Siwāk* (tooth-stick). It was highly recommended by the Prophet (peace and blessing of Allāh be upon him).

5. Sniff water into the nostrils and blow it out.

6. Wash the face from the limits of the hair to the bottom of the chin, and from ear to ear.

7. Wash the hands up to the elbows, start with the right hand first.

8. Pass wet hands over the head, and rub with wet fingers inside and outside of your ears.

9. Wash the feet up to the ankles, starting with the right foot.

If a person is wearing socks, he does not need to take them off for ablution, provided he has put them on while he had ablution. This concession is available for twenty-four hours for someone who is at home, and for three days and nights for a travelling person.

Ablution Illustrated

The washing of the parts of body in ablution may be done once, twice or three times but no more than three times. Passing wet hands over the head, inside and outside the ears and on the socks is to be done only once.

After completing the ablution say:

اَللّٰهُمَّ اجْعَلْنِيْ مِنَ التَّوَّابِيْنَ وَاجْعَلْنِيْ مِنَ الْمُتَطَهِّرِيْنَ

Ash-hadu allaa ilaaha illal-laahu wahdahoo laa shareeka lah, wa ash-hadu anna Muhammadan abduhu wa rasooluh. Allaahummaj-'alnee minat-tawwaabeena waj-'alnee minal mutatahhireen.

(I bear witness that there is no god but Allāh Alone. There is no partner unto Him. And I bear witness that Muhammad is His servant and His Messenger.)

O Allāh! Make me among those who turn to You in repentance and make me of those who strive to be pure.)

Things which invalidate Ablution

1. Passing of excrement, urine or wind.

2. Deep sleep.

3. Loss of one's senses by any means such as madness, fainting, drunkenness, or use of drugs, etc.

4. Touching the sexual organs intentionally and with naked hands.

When in doubt do not renew the ablution unless you are sure that your ablution has become invalid. However, to make a new ablution for every prayer is a matter of additional reward.

Tayammum or Dry Ablution

Tayammum is a substitute for ablution or ritual bath. It is performed in the following cases:

1. When water is not available to perform ablution or ritual bath.

2. When someone is wounded or injured or ill, and there is fear that use of water will aggravate his condition.

3. In severe cold when it is feared that use of water will cause suffering.

How to perform Tayammum

There are two ways of performing *Tayammum:*

1. Strike both your hands with fingers stretched on clean earth, raise them and blow off the excessive dust, and then pass them over your face and rub the two hands in and out up to the wrists.

2. Strike both hands on the earth, blow the excessive dust and pass them over your face. Strike the hands on earth again and rub each hand up to the elbow starting with the right hand.

After the completion say the same supplication which is mentioned above.

Prayer in Congregation

Performing the obligatory prayers in congregation is highly recommended. The Prophet (peace and blessing of Allāh be upon him) said:

"Prayer in congregation is superior by 27 degrees to prayer performed individually." *(Bukhāri and Muslim)*

Remaining away from the congregation without a valid reason is a very serious offence, as illustrated in the following *Hadith:*

Abu Hurayrah (may Allāh be pleased with him) reported that the Messenger of Allāh (peace and blessing of Allāh be upon him) said:

"By the One in Whose Hand is my soul, sometimes I intend that I ask someone to lead people in prayer while I go to the people who remain away from the congregation and burn their houses along with them with fire." *(Bukhāri and Muslim)*

When a person goes to a mosque, he should enter with his right foot first and say:

بِسْمِ اللهِ اَللّٰهُمَّ صَلِّ عَلٰى مُحَمَّدٍ ،
اَللّٰهُمَّ افْتَحْ لِيْ أَبْوَابَ رَحْمَتِكَ

Bismillaah, Allaahumma salli 'alaa Muhammad.
Allaahummaf-tah lee abwaaba rahmatik.

(In the Name of Allāh.
O Allāh! Shower blessing on Muhammad.
O Allāh! Open for me the gates of Your Mercy.)

After entering the mosque, one should perform two *Rak'ah* prayer. It is called *Tahiyyat Al-Masjid* (Salutation of the Mosque). It is a *Sunnah* recommended by the Prophet (peace and blessing of Allāh be upon him). He said: "When one of you enters the mosque, he should perform two *Rak'ah* before taking his seat." *(Bukhāri and Muslim)*

When a person is inside the mosque, he should remember that he is in the house of Allāh, which must be given its due respect. Therefore, he should sit quietly and keep himself busy in prayer, remembrance of Allāh and recitation of the Qur'ān. He should avoid raising his voice, indulging in vain talk or argument with others. According to a *Hadith,* a person who sits in the mosque waiting for the next prayer, is like the one who is performing the prayer.

While leaving the mosque, one should take out the left foot first and say:

بِسْمِ اللهِ اللّٰهُمَّ صَلِّ عَلٰى مُحَمَّدٍ،
اَللّٰهُمَّ اِنِّىْ اَسْئَلُكَ مِنْ فَضْلِكَ۔

Bismillaah, Allaahumma salli 'alaa Muhammad.
Allaahumma innee as'aluka min fadlik.

(In the Name of Allāh.
O Allāh! Shower blessing on Muhammad.
O Allāh! I am asking You for Your Grace.)

Adhān (Call to Prayer)

Adhān is instituted to call people to prayer. Whether in a mosque or in an open place, when two or more people want to perform an obligatory prayer, one of them should make the *Adhān*.

The words of *Adhān* are:

اللهُ أَكْبَرُ ، اللهُ أَكْبَرُ .

اللهُ أَكْبَرُ ، اللهُ أَكْبَرُ .

أَشْهَدُ أَنْ لَا إِلَهَ إِلَّا اللهُ ،

أَشْهَدُ أَنْ لَا إِلَهَ إِلَّا اللهُ .

أَشْهَدُ أَنَّ مُحَمَّدًا رَسُولُ اللهِ ،

أَشْهَدُ أَنَّ مُحَمَّدًا رَسُولُ اللهِ .

حَيَّ عَلَى الصَّلَاةِ ، حَيَّ عَلَى الصَّلَاةِ .

حَيَّ عَلَى الْفَلَاحِ ، حَيَّ عَلَى الْفَلَاحِ .

اللهُ أَكْبَرُ ، اللهُ أَكْبَرُ .

لَا إِلَهَ إِلَّا اللهُ .

Allaahu Akbar, Allaahu Akbar
Allāh is the Greatest, Allāh is the Greatest
Allaahu Akbar, Allaahu Akbar
Allāh is the Greatest, Allāh is the Greatest
Ash-hadu allaa ilaaha illal-laah
I bear witness that there is no god but Allāh
Ash-hadu allaa ilaaha illal-laah
I bear witness that there is no god but Allāh
Ash-hadu anna Muhammadar Rasoolul-laah

I bear witness that Muhammad is
the Messenger of Allāh
*Ash-hadu anna Muhammadar
Rasoolul-laah*
I bear witness that Muhammad is
the Messenger of Allāh
Hayya 'alas-salaah
Come to the prayer
Hayya 'alas-salaah
Come to the prayer
Hayya 'alal falaah
Come to the success
Hayya 'alai falaah
Come to the success
Allaahu Akbar, Allaahu Akbar
Allāh is the Greatest, Allāh is the Greatest
Laa ilaaha illal-laah
There is no god but Allāh.

When *Adhān* is called, those who listen to it should answer by repeating the same words except when the caller says *Hayya 'alas-salaah* and *Hayya 'alal-falaah,* the listener should say:

لَاحَوْلَ وَلَا قُوَّةَ إِلَّا بِاللهِ

Laa hawla wa laa quwwata illaa billaah.

(There is no power and no strength except with Allāh.)

When the *Adhān* is completed, the caller and the listener both should invoke the blessing of Allāh on the Prophet (peace and blessing of Allāh be upon him) as follows:

اَللّٰهُمَّ صَلِّ عَلَى مُحَمَّدٍ وَّعَلَى اٰلِ مُحَمَّدٍ كَمَا صَلَّيْتَ عَلَى إِبْرَاهِيْمَ وَعَلَى اٰلِ إِبْرَاهِيْمَ إِنَّكَ حَمِيْدٌ مَّجِيْدٌ، اَللّٰهُمَّ بَارِكْ عَلَى مُحَمَّدٍ وَّعَلَى اٰلِ مُحَمَّدٍ كَمَا بَارَكْتَ عَلَى إِبْرَاهِيْمَ وَعَلَى اٰلِ إِبْرَاهِيْمَ إِنَّكَ حَمِيْدٌ مَّجِيْدٌ

Allaahumma salli 'alaa Muhammadin wa 'alaa aali Muhammadin kamaa sallayta 'alaa Ibraaheema wa 'alaa aali Ibraaheema, innaka Hameedum Majeed.

*Allaahumma baarik 'alaa Muhammadin wa 'alaa aali
Muhammadin kamaa baarakta 'alaa Ibraaheema wa
'alaa aali Ibraaheema, innaka Hameedum Majeed.*

(O Allāh! Show mercy to Muhammad and the family of
Muhammad as You have shown mercy to Ibrahim and
the family of Ibrahim. You are indeed Praiseworthy,
Glorious. O Allāh! Bless Muhammad and the family of
Muhammad as You have blessed Ibrahim and the family
of Ibrahim. You are indeed Praiseworthy, Glorious.)

Then say the following supplication:

اَللّٰهُمَّ رَبَّ هٰذِهِ الدَّعْوَةِ التَّآمَّةِ وَالصَّلٰوةِ الْقَآئِمَةِ
أَتِ مُحَمَّدَا۟ الْوَسِيْلَةَ وَ الْفَضِيْلَةَ وَابْعَثْهُ مَقَامًا
مَّحْمُوْدَا۟ الَّذِىْ وَعَدْتَهُ

*Allaahumma Rabba haadhihid-da 'watit-taammati
was-salaatil-gaa'imati aati Muhammada nil-waseelata
wal-fadeelata wab 'athhu maqaamam mahmooda
nil-ladhee wa 'adtahu.*

(O Allāh! The Lord of this perfect call and the prayer to
be established, grant Muhammad the *Wasilah* and
eminence, and raise him to the praiseworthy position
which You promised him.)

The Prophet (peace and blessing of Allāh be upon him) recommended it. *(Bukhāri)*

Sa'd bin Abi Waqqās (may Allāh be pleased with him) reported that the Messenger of Allāh (peace and blessing of Allāh be upon him) said:

"When a person listens to the caller, then says the following supplication, his sins will be forgiven:

Ash-hadu allaa ilaaha illal-laahu wahdahu laa shareeka lahu, wa anna Muhammadan 'abduhu wa rasooluhu. Radeetu billaahi rabban wa bi Muhammadin rasoolan, wa bil-Islaami deena.

(I bear witness that there is no god but Allāh Alone, there is no partner with Him, and that Muhammad is His servant and His Messenger. I have chosen Allāh as Lord, Muhammad as Messenger and Islam as religion.)
(Muslim)

Iqāmah

The *Iqāmah* is called to let it be known that the prayer is about to begin. It differs slightly from the Adhān.

The words of the *Iqāmah* are:

Allaahu Akbar, Allaahu Akbar   اَللهُ اَكْبَرُ ، اَللهُ اَكْبَرُ
Allāh is the Greatest, Allāh is the Greatest

Ash-hadu allaa ilaaha illal-laah   اَشْهَدُ اَنْ لَّا اِلٰهَ اِلَّا اللهُ
I bear witness that there is no god but Allāh

Ash-hadu anna Muhammadar Rasoolul-laah   اَشْهَدُ اَنَّ مُحَمَّدًا رَسُوْلُ اللهِ
I bear witness that Muhammad is the Messenger of Allāh

Hayya 'alas-salaah
Come to the prayer
Hayya 'alal-falaah   حَيَّ عَلَى الصَّلَاةِ   حَيَّ عَلَى الْفَلَاحِ
Come to the success

Qadqaamatis-salaah, Qad qaamatis-salaah   قَدْ قَامَتِ الصَّلٰوةُ ، قَدْ قَامَتِ الصَّلٰوةُ
The prayer is being established
The prayer is being established

Allaahu Akbar, Allaahu Akbar   اَللهُ اَكْبَرُ ، اَللهُ اَكْبَرُ
Allāh is the Greatest, Allāh is the Greatest

Laa ilaaha illal-laah   لَآ اِلٰهَ اِلَّا اللهُ ۔
There is no god but Allāh.

Number of Rak'ah in Obligatory Prayers

1. *Fajr* (dawn) prayer has only two *Rak'ah*. The *Imām* reads in them Surat *Al-Fātihah* (Opening Chapter) and a long chapter or portion of the Qur'ān loudly.

2. *Zuhr* (noon) prayer has four *Rak'ah*. Reading is done in them quietly.

3. *Asr* (afternoon) prayer also has four *Rak'ah* and reading is done quietly.

4. *Maghrib* (sunset) prayer consists of three *Rak'ah*. In the first two *Rak'ah*, the Imām recites *Al-Fātihah* and a small chapter of the Qur'ān loudly; and in the third *Rak'ah*, only *Al-Fātihah* is read quietly.

5. *Isha'* (night) prayer has four Rak'ah. In the first two, Surat Al-Fātihah and a medium chapter of the Qur'ān are recited loudly; and in the last two, only Al-Fātihah is read quietly.

When the *Imām* recites loudly, the people behind him should recite *Al-Fātihah* only quietly; and when he recites quietly, those behind him should recite quietly as well.

However, in the first two *Rak'ah* of *Zuhr* and *'Asr* prayer, they should add a chapter or some verses from the Holy Qur'ān after Surat *Al-Fātihah*. According to some scholars, the people behind an *Imām* do not need to read anything and should remain silent.

When a person joins the congregation after the *Imām* has started, he should join with saying *Allāhu Akbar,* and follow the Imām. If he has missed some *Rak'ah,* he should complete it after the Imam has completed the prayer by *Taslim*. According to a *Hadith,* if a person joins the congregation while the *Imām* was in *Ruku',* he should count that *Rak'ah,* but if he joins the *Imām* after he has done the *Ruku',* then that *Rak'ah* should not be counted.

How Prayer is performed

1. Stand straight facing the *Qiblah*. Keep your feet straight and toes directed towards the *Qiblah*.

2. Make intention of the prayer you want to perform e.g., *Zuhr, 'Asr*, etc., *Fard* or *Nafl*.

3. Raise your hands to the shoulders or to the ears, keep the fingers stretched and make the palms face the *Qiblah*. Say *Allāhu Akbar* (Allāh is the Greatest). This is *Takbir Tahrimah*. Now your prayer has started.

4. Place your right hand over the left and put them together on your chest, below the chest or above the navel.

5. Read any of the following supplications quietly:

①

سُبْحَانَكَ اللّٰهُمَّ وَبِحَمْدِكَ وَتَبَارَكَ اسْمُكَ
وَتَعَالَى جَدُّكَ وَلَا إِلٰهَ غَيْرُكَ.

Subhaanakal-laahumma wa bihamdika wa tabaarakas-muka wa ta 'aalaa jadduka wa laa ilaaha ghayruka.

(Glory be to You, O Allāh, and praise is due to You. Blessed is Your Name, and exalted is Your Majesty and there is no god but You.)

اَللّٰهُمَّ بَاعِدْ بَيْنِى وَبَيْنَ خَطَايَاىَ كَمَا بَاعَدْتَ بَيْنَ الْمَشْرِقِ وَالْمَغْرِبِ اَللّٰهُمَّ نَقِّنِى مِنْ خَطَايَاىَ كَمَا يُنَقَّى الثَّوْبُ الْأَبْيَضُ مِنَ الدَّنَسِ اَللّٰهُمَّ اغْسِلْ خَطَايَاىَ بِالْمَاءِ وَالثَّلْجِ وَالْبَرَدِ

Allaahumma baa'id baynee wa bayna khataayaaya kamaa baa 'adta baynal-mashriqi wal-maghribi. Allaahumma naqqinee min khataayaaya kamaa yunaqqath-thawbul-abyadu minad-danase. Allaahummagh-sil khataayaaya bil-maa'i wath-thalji wal-barad.

(O Allāh, make a distance between me and my sins as You have made the distance between east and west. O Allāh, purify me from the sins as the white garment is purified from the dirt. O Allāh, wash away my sins with water, snow and hailstones.)

Seek refuge with Allāh from Satan by saying:

اَعُوْذُ بِاللهِ مِنَ الشَّيْطٰنِ الرَّجِيْمِ

A'oodhu billaahi minash-Shaytaanir-rajeem.
(I seek refuge with Allāh from the cursed Satan.)

3

Recite *Al-Fātihah*, the opening chapter of the Qur'ān:

بِسْمِ اللهِ الرَّحْمٰنِ الرَّحِيْمِ

اَلْحَمْدُ لِلّٰهِ رَبِّ الْعٰلَمِيْنَ ۝ الرَّحْمٰنِ الرَّحِيْمِ ۝ مٰلِكِ يَوْمِ الدِّيْنِ ۝
اِيَّاكَ نَعْبُدُ وَ اِيَّاكَ نَسْتَعِيْنُ ۝ اِهْدِنَا الصِّرَاطَ الْمُسْتَقِيْمَ ۝
صِرَاطَ الَّذِيْنَ اَنْعَمْتَ عَلَيْهِمْ لَغَيْرِ الْمَغْضُوْبِ عَلَيْهِمْ وَلَا الضَّآلِّيْنَ ۝

Bismillaahir-Rahmaanir-Raheem.
Alhamdu lillaahi Rabbil-'aalameen. Ar-Rahmaanir-
Raheem. Maaliki yawmid-deen. Iyyaaka na'budu
wa iyyaaka nasta'een. Ihdinas-siraatal-mustaqeem.
Siraatal-ladheena an'amta 'alayhim, ghayril-magh-
doobi 'alayhim wa lad-daalleen.

In the Name of Allāh,
the Most Gracious, the Most Merciful.
All the praises and thanks be to Allāh,
the Lord of the Worlds.
The Most Gracious, the Most Merciful.
The Only Owner of the Day of Recompense.
Only You we worship, and only You we ask for help.
Guide us to the Straight Path.
The Path of those on whom You have bestowed
Your grace, not of those who earned Your anger,
nor of those who went astray.

At the end of Surat *Al-Fātihah,* say *Āmeen.*

④ Recite any *Surah* or a few verses from the Qur'ān.

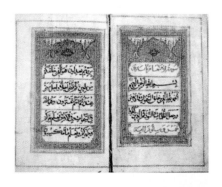

5 **Raise your both hands to the shoulders or to the ears,**

Say *Allāhu Akbar* and bow down in *Ruku'*. Place your hands on both knees with fingers spread out. Make sure that your back and head are at the same level.

Some scholars do not consider it necessary to raise hands while going to *Ruku'* or rising from it.

6 Say:

سُبْحَانَ رَبِّيَ الْعَظِيمِ

Subhaana Rabbiyal-'Azeem
(Glory be to my Lord, the Great)

This should be said at least three times. Or say:

سُبُّوحٌ قُدُّوسٌ رَبُّ الْمَلَائِكَةِ وَالرُّوحِ

Subboohun Quddoosun, Rabbull-malaa'ikati war-rooh.
(All-Glorious, All-Holy, the Lord of angels and the Spirit.)

7 **Rise from the *Ruku'***
and raise your hands, as you did
previously, saying:

سَمِعَ اللهُ لِمَنْ حَمِدَهُ

Sami allaahu liman hamidah.
(Allāh listened to one who
praised Him.)

Then say:

رَبَّنَا وَلَكَ الْحَمْدُ حَمْدًا
كَثِيرًا طَيِّبًا مُبَارَكًا فِيهِ

*Rabbanaa wa lakal-hamdu hamdan katheeran tayyiban
mubaarakan feeh.*

(Our Lord, to You be the praise, the praise in abundance,
pure and blessed.)

8 **Saying *Allāhu Akbar,* bow down for prostration.**

Place the forehead, nose, both palms and knees on the
ground, and keep the underarms open. Place the hands in
line with the shoulders and ears. Keep the fingers straight
and together facing the *Qiblah*. The toes should also be
facing the *Qiblah*.

9 **Say three times at least:**

سُبْحَانَ رَبِّيَ الْأَعْلَى

Subhaana Rabbiyal-A'laa.
(Glory be to my Lord, the Most High.) Or say:

سُبْحَانَكَ اللّٰهُمَّ رَبَّنَا وَبِحَمْدِكَ اللّٰهُمَّ اغْفِرْ لِي

Subhaanakal-lahumma Rabbanaa wa bihamdika, Allaahummagh-firlee.

(Glory be to You, O Allāh, our Lord. Praise is due to You. O Allāh, forgive me.)

10 **Raise your head**

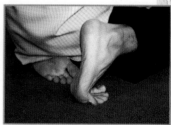

Saying *Allāhu Akbar.* Fold your left leg and sit on it and keep Your right foot upright with toes turned to the *Qiblah.* Place the open hands on the thighs.

11 **While sitting in this position say:**

اَللّٰهُمَّ اغْفِرْ لِي وَارْحَمْنِي وَعَافِنِي وَاهْدِنِي وَارْزُقْنِي

Allaahummagh-fir lee war-hamnee wa'aafinee wah-dinee war-zuqnee.

(O Allāh, forgive me, have mercy on me, grant me well-being, guide me and grant me provision.)

12 Saying *Allāhu Akbar*, go to a second prostration in the same way as you did for the first one.

13 Saying *Allāhu Akbar*, rise from the prostration and sand up for the second *Rak'ah*. Some scholars recommend that before standing one should sit for a short while. It is called *Jalsat-ul-Istirāhah* (sitting to rest).

14 Start the second *Rak'ah* by reciting *Al-Fātihah* and repeat all the actions of the first *Rak'ah*.

15 At the end of the second *Rak'ah*, sit as you did between two prostrations and read *Tashahhud* as follows:

اَلتَّحِيَّاتُ لِلهِ وَالصَّلَوَاتُ وَالطَّيِّبَاتُ السَّلَامُ عَلَيْكَ اَيُّهَا النَّبِيُّ وَرَحْمَةُ اللهِ وَبَرَكَاتُهُ اَلسَّلَامُ عَلَيْنَا وَعَلَى عِبَادِ اللهِ الصَّالِحِينَ اَشْهَدُ اَنْ لَّا إِلهَ إِلَّا اللهُ وَاَشْهَدُ اَنَّ مُحَمَّدًا عَبْدُهُ وَرَسُولُهُ

At-tahiyyaatu lillaahi was-salawaatu wat-tayyibaatu, as-salaamu 'alayka ayyuhan-Nabiyyu wa rahmatul-laahi wa barakaatuhu, as-salaamu 'alaynaa wa 'ala 'ibaadil-laahis-saaliheen. Ash-hadu allaa ilaaha illal-laahu wa ash-hadu anna Muhammadan 'abduhu wa rasooluhu.

(All praise, all worship and all good things are for Allāh. Peace be upon you, O Prophet, and Allāh's mercy and

His blessings. Peace be upon us, and all righteous servants of Allāh. I bear witness that there is no god but Allāh and I bear witness that Muhammad is His servant and His Messenger.)

While reading *Tashahhud,* you should raise the index finger of your right hand slightly and return it to its previous position after you have finished saying it.

16 **Saying** *Allāhu Akbar,* **rise for the third** *Rak'ah* and raise your hands as you did in the beginning of the prayer. Some scholars do not consider it necessary. Do exactly as you did in the previous *Rak'ah* except that you do not need to read another *Surah* after *Al-Fātihah.* If it is a four-*Rak'ah* prayer, do in the fourth *Rak'ah* as you did in the third one.

17 **When you have completed your prayer,** sit as prescribed in 10 or if you can sit on the ground pulling the left foot out and keeping the right one upright.

8 **Read the** *Tashahhud* **as mentioned in 15,** then invoke the blessing of Allāh on the Prophet by reading the following:

اَللّٰهُمَّ صَلِّ عَلٰى مُحَمَّدٍ وَّعَلٰى اٰلِ مُحَمَّدٍ كَمَا صَلَّيْتَ عَلٰى اِبْرَاهِيْمَ وَعَلٰى اٰلِ اِبْرَاهِيْمَ اِنَّكَ حَمِيْدٌ مَّجِيْدٌ، اَللّٰهُمَّ بَارِكْ عَلٰى مُحَمَّدٍ وَّعَلٰى اٰلِ مُحَمَّدٍ كَمَا بَارَكْتَ عَلٰى اِبْرَاهِيْمَ وَعَلٰى اٰلِ اِبْرَاهِيْمَ اِنَّكَ حَمِيْدٌ مَّجِيْدٌ

Allaahumma salli ʿalaa Muhammadin wa ʿalaa aali Muhammadin kamaa sallayta ʿalaa Ibraaheema wa ʿalaa aali Ibraaheema, innaka Hameedum Majeed.

Allaahumma baarik ʿalaa Muhammadin wa ʿalaa aali Muhammadin kamaa baarakata ʿalaa Ibraaheema wa ʿalaa aali Ibraaheema, innaka Hameedum Majeed.

(O Allāh! Show mercy to Muhammad and the family of Muhammad as You have shown mercy to Ibrahim and the family of Ibrahim. You are indeed Praiseworthy, Glorious.
O Allāh! Bless Muhammad and the family of Muhammad as You have blessed Ibrahim and the family of Ibrahim. You are indeed Praiseworthy, Glorious.)

19 **After that read any supplication you like,** but below are some which are recommended by the Prophet (peace and blessing of Allāh be upon him):

اَللّٰهُمَّ اِنِّيْ ظَلَمْتُ نَفْسِيْ ظُلْمًا كَثِيْرًا وَّلَا يَغْفِرُ
الذُّنُوْبَ اِلَّا اَنْتَ فَاغْفِرْ لِيْ مَغْفِرَةً مِّنْ عِنْدِكَ وَارْحَمْنِيْ
اِنَّكَ اَنْتَ الْغَفُوْرُ الرَّحِيْمُ

*Allaahumma innee zalamtu nafsee zulman katheeran
wa laa yaghfirudh-dhunooba illaa Anta faghfir lee
maghfiratam-min 'indika war-hamnee innaka
Antal Ghafoor-ur-Raheem.*

(O Allāh, I have wronged myself a great deal, and no one
forgives sins except You, so forgive me with a forgiveness
from You and have mercy on me. Surely, You are the Most
Forgiving, the Most Merciful.)   *(Bukhāri and Muslim)*

اَللّٰهُمَّ اغْفِرْ لِيْ مَا قَدَّمْتُ وَمَا اَخَّرْتُ وَمَا اَسْرَرْتُ
وَمَا اَعْلَنْتُ وَمَا اَسْرَفْتُ وَمَا اَنْتَ اَعْلَمُ بِهِ مِنِّيْ اَنْتَ
الْمُقَدِّمُ وَاَنْتَ الْمُؤَخِّرُ لَا اِلٰهَ اِلَّا اَنْتَ

*Allaahummagh fir lee maa qaddamtu wa maa akhkhartu
wa maa asrartu wa maa a'lantu wa maa asraftu wa
maa Anta a'lamu bihi minnee, Antal-Muqaddimu wa
Antal-Mu'akhkhiru laa ilaaha illaa Anta.*

(O Allāh, forgive my past and later sins, and what I did in private and what I did in public, and what I have exceeded in, and what You know better than me. You are the Promoter and the Retarder. There is no god but You.)
(Muslim)

20 **Turning your face to the right side say:**

اَلسَّلَامُ عَلَيْكُمْ وَرَحْمَةُ اللهِ

As-salaamu 'alaykum wa rahmatullaah.
(Peace be on you, and Allāh's mercy.)

21 **Then turn your face to the left and say:**

اَلسَّلَامُ عَلَيْكُمْ وَرَحْمَةُ اللهِ

As-salaamu 'alaykum wa rahmatullaah.
(Peace be on you and Allāh's mercy.)

This is called *Taslim,* by which the prayer ends.

Sujud As-Sahw
(Prostrations of Forgetfulness)

These are two prostrations, which are performed to make up for some mistakes during the prayer. However, if a person has missed out some obligatory act, his prayer will be null and void. Sujud As-Sahw are made in the following cases:

1. When a person does something extra, above what was required such as he performs five *Rak'ah* instead of four or three *Rak'ah* instead of two. If he remembers before final sitting, he should stop from further action and complete the prayer and make *Sujud As-Sahw*. But if he realizes his mistake after he has already sat for *Taslim,* he should continue and complete his prayer. He should also make *Sujud As-Sahw.*

2. When a person ended his prayer with *Taslim* before doing the required number of *Rak'ah*. He should complete the required number and make *Sujud As-Sahw.*

3. When a person forgets some unessential act such as sitting after two *Rak'ah* for *Tashahhud* while performing a three- or four-*Rak'ah* prayer, he should continue and make Sujud *As-Sahw* at the end.

4. When a person is in doubt concerning the number of *Rak'ah* he has performed, he should take the number he feels more certain about and continue. After completing the prayer, he should make *Sujud As-Sahw*. However, if the number of *Rak'ah* is not clear to him, then he should take the minimum number and complete his prayer, and make *Sujud As-Sahw*.

Sujud As-Sahw are performed at the end of the prayer either before or after *Taslim*. They should be made before Taslim if something was missed and in the case of doubts where there was no likelihood of one side being certain. They should be made after *Taslim* if some extra act was done, and in the case of doubts when one side was more likely than the other was. There is no special supplication or *Sujud As-Sahw*. The same *Du'a* which is read in *Sujud* should be read in *Sujud As-Sahw* as well.

After the Prayer

After completing the prayer, say *Allāhu Akbar*
Then say three times:

أَسْتَغْفِرُاللَّه

Astaghfirul-laah:

(I seek the forgiveness of Allāh),

then say:

اَللّٰهُمَّ اَنْتَ السَّلَامُ وَمِنْكَ السَّلَامُ تَبَارَكْتَ
يَاذَا الْجَلَالِ وَالْإِكْرَامِ۔

Allaahumma Antas-Salaamu wa minkas-salaam.
Tabaarakta yaa Dhal-Jalaali wal-Ikraam.

(O Allāh, You are the Peace, and from You comes the
Peace. You are Blessed, O the Sublime and the
Honourable One.)

Below are some other supplications recommended by the
Prophet (peace and blessing of Allāh be upon him):

لَا اِلٰهَ اِلَّا اللّٰهُ وَحْدَهُ لَا شَرِيْكَ لَهُ لَهُ الْمُلْكُ وَلَهُ الْحَمْدُ
وَهُوَ عَلٰى كُلِّ شَىْءٍ قَدِيْرُ۔ اَللّٰهُمَّ لَا مَانِعَ لِمَا اَعْطَيْتَ وَلَا
مُعْطِىَ لِمَا مَنَعْتَ وَلَا يَنْفَعُ ذَا الْجَدِّ مِنْكَ الْجَدُّ۔

*Laa ilaaha illal-laahu wahdahu laa shareeka lahu,
lahul-mulku wa lahul-hamdu wa Huwa 'alaa
kulli shay'in Qadeer.*

*Allāhumma laa maani'a limaa a'tayta wa laa mu'tiya
limaa mana'ta wa laa yanfa'u dhal-jaddi minkal-jadd.*

(There is no god except Allāh, the One. There is no
partner with Him. To Him belong the Kingdom and the
Praise, and He has Power over all things.)

O Allāh, none can withhold what You have conferred,
and none can confer what You have withheld. A fortune
does not benefit its owner against You.)

(Bukhāri andMuslim)

لَا إِلٰهَ إِلَّا اللهُ وَحْدَهُ لَا شَرِيكَ لَهُ لَهُ الْمُلْكُ وَلَهُ الْحَمْدُ
وَهُوَ عَلَى كُلِّ شَيْءٍ قَدِيرٌ، لَاحَوْلَ وَلَاقُوَّةَ إِلَّا بِاللهِ لَا إِلٰهَ
إِلَّا اللهُ وَلَا نَعْبُدُ إِلَّا إِيَّاهُ، لَهُ النِّعْمَةُ وَلَهُ الْفَضْلُ وَلَهُ
الثَّنَاءُ الْحَسَنُ، لَا إِلٰهَ إِلَّا اللهُ مُخْلِصِينَ لَهُ الدِّينَ وَلَوْ
كَرِهَ الْكَافِرُونَ-

*Laa ilaaha illal-laahu wahdahu laa shareeka lahu,
lahul-mulku wa lahul-hamdu wa Huwa 'alaa kulli
shay'in Qadeer. Laa hawla wa laa quwwata illaa
billaah. Laa ilaaha illal-laahu wa laa na'budu illaa
iyyaahu, lahun-ni'matu wa lahul-fadlu wa lahuth-
thanaa'ul-hasanu. Laa ilaaha illal-laahu mukhliseena
lahud-deena wa law karihal-kaafiroon.*

(There is no god but Allāh, the One. There is no partner with Him. To Him belongs the sovereignty, and to Him is due the praise, and He has power over all things. There is no strength and no power except with Allāh.

We do not worship any but Him. To Him belong the Bounty, the Grace and the best praise. There is no god except Allāh. We are sincerely devoted to Him even if the unbelievers dislike it.)   *(Ahmad and Muslim)*

رَبِّ اَعِنِّيْ عَلٰى ذِكْرِكَ وَ شُكْرِكَ وَ حُسْنِ عِبَادَتِكَ.

Rabbi a'innee alaa dhikrika wa shukrika wa husni 'ibaadatika.

(My Lord, help me in remembering You, thanking You and worshipping You in the best way.)
(Ahmad, Abu Dāwud and An-Nasa'i)

The Verse of the Throne:

اَللّٰهُ لَآ اِلٰهَ اِلَّا هُوَ ۚ اَلْحَيُّ الْقَيُّوْمُ ۚ لَا تَأْخُذُهٗ سِنَةٌ وَّلَا نَوْمٌ ۚ لَهٗ مَا فِي السَّمٰوٰتِ وَمَا فِي الْاَرْضِ ۗ مَنْ ذَا الَّذِيْ يَشْفَعُ عِنْدَهٗٓ اِلَّا بِاِذْنِهٖ ۚ يَعْلَمُ مَا بَيْنَ اَيْدِيْهِمْ وَمَا خَلْفَهُمْ ۚ وَلَا يُحِيْطُوْنَ بِشَيْءٍ مِّنْ عِلْمِهٖٓ اِلَّا بِمَا شَآءَ ۚ وَسِعَ كُرْسِيُّهُ السَّمٰوٰتِ وَالْاَرْضَ ۚ وَلَا يَـُٔوْدُهٗ حِفْظُهُمَا ۚ وَهُوَ الْعَلِيُّ الْعَظِيْمُ

Allaahu laa-ilaaha illaa Huwal-Hayyul-Qayyoom. Laa ta'khudhu-hu sinatun wa laa nawm. Lahu maa fis-samaawaati wa maa fil-ard. Man dhal-ladhee yashfa'u 'indahu illaa bi idhnihi, ya 'lamu maa bayna aydeehim wa maa khalfahum, wa laa yuheetoona bi shay'im-min 'ilmihi illaa bimaa shaa'a, wasi'a kursiyyuhus-samaawaati wal-arda wa laa ya'ooduhu hifzuhumaa, wa Huwal- Aliyyul-'Azeem.

(Allāh, there is no God except Him, the Living, the Self-Sustaining Eternal. Neither slumber nor sleep seizes Him. To Him belongs all that is in the heavens and on earth. Who is there who can intercede in His presence except as He permits? He knows what is before them and behind them. They cannot compass anything of His knowledge except as He wills. His Throne encompasses the heavens and the earth and He feels no fatigue in guarding and pre-serving them. He is the Most High, the Supreme.)

Say each of the following 33 times:

Subhaanal-laah
(Glory to Allāh)

سُبْحَانَ اللهِ

Alhamdu lillaah
(Praise be to Allāh)

اَلْحَمْدُ لِلّٰهِ

Allaahu Akbar
(Allāh is the Greatest)

اَللهُ أَكْبَرُ

To complete the hundred, say:

لَا إِلَهَ إِلَّا اللهُ وَحْدَهُ لَا شَرِيكَ لَهُ لَهُ الْمُلْكُ وَلَهُ الْحَمْدُ وَهُوَ عَلَى كُلِّ شَيْءٍ قَدِيرٌ۔

Laa ilaaha illal-laahu, wahdahu laa shareeka lahu, lahul-mulku wa lahul-hamdu, wa Huwa 'alaa kulli shay'in Qadeer.

(There is no god except Allah, the One. There is no partner with Him. To Him belong the Sovereignty and the Praise, and He has Power over all things.) *(Muslim)*

SUNNAH
(Supererogatory) Prayers

They are of two types:

i) *Sunan Mu'akkadah*

These are the prayers which have been emphasised by the Prophet (peace and blessing of Allāh be upon him).

They are as follows:

1. Two *Rak'ah* before *Fajr* prayer.

A'ishah (may Allāh be pleased with her) said that the Messenger of Allāh (peace and blessing of Allāh be upon him) was not so keen on observing any supererogatory prayer as he was in observing two *Rak'ahs* before *Fajr*. *(Bukhāri and Muslim)*

2. Two or four *Rak'ah* before *Zuhr* prayer.
3. Two *Rak'ah* after *Zuhr* prayer.
4. Two *Rak'ah* after *Maghrib* prayer.
5. Two *Rak'ah* after *'Isha'* prayer.

ii) *Sunan Ghair Mu'akkadah*

These are four *Rak'ah* before *'Asr* prayer. Besides, the Prophet (peace and blessing of Allāh be upon him) recommended, without emphasising, performing of prayer between the *Adhān* and *Iqāmah* of every prayer.

WITR

This is a *Sunnah Mu'akkadah* prayer, but some scholars consider it as *Wājib*.

The number of Rak'ah in this prayer has to be odd, and it is performed after the *'Isha'* prayer.

There are three different ways of performing three *Rak'ah Witr*:

i) First perform two *Rak'ah* and after that perform another one.

ii) Perform all three *Rak'ah* together without sitting after two.

iii) Do it like *Maghrib* prayer, i.e, sit after two, then after *Tashahhud* stand for the third *Rak'ah*.

Qunut

Qunut is a supplication, which is said during the *Witr* prayer. It could be said before or after the *Ruku'* of the last *Rak'ah*. There are two versions of *Qunut*:

اَللّٰهُمَّ اهْدِنِيْ فِيْمَنْ هَدَيْتَ وَعَافِنِيْ فِيْمَنْ عَافَيْتَ
وَتَوَلَّنِيْ فِيْمَنْ تَوَلَّيْتَ وَبَارِكْ لِيْ فِيْمَآ اَعْطَيْتَ وَقِنِيْ شَرَّ
مَا قَضَيْتَ فَاِنَّكَ تَقْضِيْ وَلَا يُقْضٰى عَلَيْكَ اِنَّهٗ لَايَذِلُّ
مَنْ وَّالَيْتَ وَلَا يَعِزُّ مَنْ عَادَيْتَ تَبَارَكْتَ رَبَّنَا وَتَعَالَيْتَ
وَصَلَّى اللهُ عَلَى النَّبِيِّ مُحَمَّدٍ

Allaahummah-dinee feeman hadayt, wa 'aafinee feeman 'aafayt, wa tawallanee feeman tawallayt, wa baarik lee' feemaa a'tayt, wa qinee sharra maa qadayt. Fa innaka taqdee wa laa yuqdaa 'alayk, innahu laa yadhillu manwaalayt, wa laa ya 'izzu man 'aadayt. Tabaarakta Rabbanaa wa ta 'aalayt. Wa sallallaahu 'alan-Nabiyyi Muhammad.

(O Allāh, guide me among those You have guided. Grant me safety among those whom You have granted safety. Take care of me among those whom You have taken into care. Bless me in what You have given. Protect me from the evil You have decreed. For You decree, and nothing is decreed upon You. No one who is in Your care is humiliated and there is no honour for the one whom You take as enemy. Blessed and Exalted

are You, O our Lord. May Allāh show mercy on the
Prophet Muhammad.)
(Abu Dāwud, An-Nasa'i, At-Tirmidhi and Ibn Mājah)

(B)

اَللّٰهُمَّ اِنَّا نَسْتَعِيْنُكَ وَ نَسْتَغْفِرُكَ وَنَسْتَهْدِيْكَ، وَنُؤْمِنُ

بِكَ وَنَتُوْبُ اِلَيْكَ، وَنَتَوَكَّلُ عَلَيْكَ، وَنُثْنِيْ عَلَيْكَ الْخَيْرَ كُلَّهُ،

وَنَشْكُرُكَ وَلَا نَكْفُرُكَ، وَنَخْلَعُ وَنَتْرُكُ مَنْ يَّفْجُرُكَ

اَللّٰهُمَّ اِيَّاكَ نَعْبُدُ، وَلَكَ نُصَلِّيْ وَ نَسْجُدُ، وَاِلَيْكَ

نَسْعٰى وَ نَحْفِدُ نَرْجُوْا رَحْمَتَكَ وَ نَخْشٰى عَذَابَكَ، اِنَّ

عَذَابَكَ بِالْكَافِرِيْنَ مُلْحِقٌ

*Allaahumma innaa nasta'eenuka wa nastaghfiruka wa
nastahdeeka, wa nu'minu bika wa natoobu ilayka, wa
natawkkalu 'alayka, wa nuthnee 'alaykal-khayra
kullahu, wanashkuruka wa laa nakfuruka, wa nakhla'u
wa natruku man-yafjuruka.
Allaahumma iyyaaka na'budu, wa laka nusallee wa
nasjudu, wa ilayka nas'aa wa nahfidu narjoo
rahmataka wa nakhshaa 'adhaabaka, inna 'adhaabaka
bil-kaafireena mulhiq.*

(O Allāh, we seek help from You. We seek Your forgiveness. We seek Your guidance. We believe in You, turn in repentance to You and place our trust in You. We laud Your Name. We thank You and do not show ingratitude. We renounce and turn away from him who disobeys You. O Allāh, we worship You. To You we pray and prostrate, and to You we hasten to work and to serve You. We beg for Your mercy and fear Your punishment. Your punishment will overtake the unbelievers.)

Friday Prayer

Friday prayer is obligatory for every Muslim male who has no valid excuse. The following people are not obliged to go for Friday prayer, but if they do, they will be rewarded:

1. Women,

2. Children,

3. A sick person,

4. A man on journey,

5. People who are confined in their homes because of bad weather or any other reason.

These people should observe *Zuhr* prayer instead.

Preparation for Friday Prayer

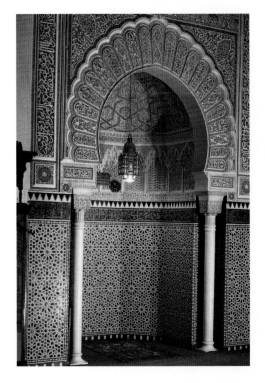

It is desirable to take a bath on Friday, put on clean clothes, wear perfume and then proceed to the mosque. One should proceed as early as possible. When in the mosque, offer as many *Rak'ah* of prayer as you can before the sermon starts.

How Friday Prayer is performed

The Friday prayer is composed of a sermon and two-*Rak'ah* prayer. The *Imām* delivers the sermon which includes the praise of Allāh, salutation for the Prophet and admonition for the congregation. The sermon has two parts divided by a sitting between them. The sermon should be short and comprehensive.

During the sermon, the congregation is required to sit quietly and listen attentively. Talking during the sermon is forbidden.

After the sermon, the *Imām* leads the congregation in two-*Rak'ah* prayer in which the *Qur'ān* is recited aloud.

After the prayer, two or more *Rak'ah* supererogatory prayer can be performed. However it is desirable to do it at home.

'EID PRAYER

'Eid prayer, like Friday prayer, is also composed of a sermon and two *Rak'ah* prayer, but on 'Eid the sermon follows the prayer. The 'Eid prayer also has some additional *Takbirs*. They are twelve according to one group and six according to another.

'Eid prayer should be performed, if possible, in an open place. Its time is after the sun has risen in the sky to a height of about three metres. There is no *Nafl* prayer before or after the 'Eid prayer.

It is desirable to take a bath, put on new and clean clothes and wear perfume. It is *Sunnah* to go to the place of worship from one way and return from another. On the way to the place of worship, the following words of praise and glorification of Allāh should be repeated:

اَللّٰهُ اَكْبَرُ، اَللّٰهُ اَكْبَرُ، لَا اِلٰهَ اِلَّا اللّٰهُ، اَللّٰهُ اَكْبَرُ،
اَللّٰهُ اَكْبَرُ، وَلِلّٰهِ الْحَمْدُ

Allaahu Akbar, Allaahu Akbar, laa ilaaha illal-laah,
Allaahu Akbar, Allaahu Akbar, wa lillaahil-hamd.

(Allāh is the Greatest, Allāh is the Greatest. There is no
god except Allāh. Allāh is the Greatest,
Allāh is the Greatest. For Allāh is the praise.)

اَللّٰهُ اَكْبَرُ كَبِيْرًا، وَالْحَمْدُ لِلّٰهِ كَثِيْرًا، وَسُبْحَانَ اللّٰهِ
بُكْرَةً وَّاَصِيْلًا

Allaahu Akbar kabeera, wal-hamdu lillaahi katheera,
wa subhaanal-laahi bukratan wa aseela.

(Allāh is surely Greatest. For Allāh is abundant praise.
Glory be to Allāh day and night.)

لَا اِلٰهَ اِلَّا اللّٰهُ وَحْدَهُ، صَدَقَ وَعْدَهُ، وَنَصَرَ عَبْدَهُ
وَاَعَزَّ جُنْدَهُ وَهَزَمَ الْاَحْزَابَ وَحْدَهُ.

Laa ilaaha illal-lahhu wahdah, sadaqa wa'dah, wa
nasara 'abdah, wa a'azza jundahu wa hazamal-
ahzaaba wahdah.

(There is no god but Allāh, the One. He fulfilled His promise, supported His servant, strengthened His army and He Alone inflicted defeat on the allied enemies.)

لَا اِلٰهَ اِلَّا اللهُ، وَلَا نَعْبُدُ اِلَّا اِيَّاهُ، مُخْلِصِيْنَ لَهُ الدِّيْنَ وَلَوْ كَرِهَ الْكَافِرُوْنَ۔

Laa ilaaha illal-laah, wa laa na 'budu illaa iy yaah, mukhliseena lahud-deena wa law karihal-kaafiroon.

(There is no god except Allāh. We worship none but Him, with sincere devotion though the disbelievers may resent it.)

اَللّٰهُمَّ صَلِّ عَلٰى مُحَمَّدٍ وَّعَلٰى اٰلِ مُحَمَّدٍ كَمَا صَلَّيْتَ عَلٰى اِبْرَاهِيْمَ وَعَلٰى اٰلِ اِبْرَاهِيْمَ اِنَّكَ حَمِيْدٌ مَّجِيْدٌ، اَللّٰهُمَّ بَارِكْ عَلٰى مُحَمَّدٍ وَّعَلٰى اٰلِ مُحَمَّدٍ كَمَا بَارَكْتَ عَلٰى اِبْرَاهِيْمَ وَعَلٰى اٰلِ اِبْرَاهِيْمَ اِنَّكَ حَمِيْدٌ مَّجِيْدٌ

Allaahumma salli 'alaa Muhammadin wa 'alaa aali Muhammadin kamaa sallayta 'alaa Ibraaheema wa 'alaa aali Ibraaheema, innaka Hameedum Majeed.

Allaahumma baarik 'alaa Muhammadin wa 'alaa aali Muhammadin kamaa baarakata 'alaa Ibraaheema wa 'alaa aali Ibraaheema, innaka Hameedum Majeed.

(O Allāh! Show mercy to Muhammad and the family of
Muhammad as You have shown mercy to Ibrahim
and the family of Ibrahim. You are indeed Praiseworthy, Glorious.)

O Allāh! Bless Muhammad and the family of Muhammad
as You have blessed Ibrahim and the family of lbrahim.
You are indeed Praiseworthy, Glorious.)

Funeral Prayer

Funeral prayer is *Fard Kifāyah,* a collective obligation for the community as a whole. If a few people perform it, the rest of the community will be free of the obligation, but if nobody does it, then the whole community will be accountable for it.

Since it is a prayer, all the conditions of normal prayer will apply to it. However, the funeral prayer does not have Ruku' or *Sujud.* It consists of mainly prayer for the deceased person. The body of the deceased should be placed in front of the row. The *Imām* will stand near the head if the deceased is a man, and in the middle if it is the body of a woman. The people will make rows behind the *Imām.* The rows should be in odd numbers.

How to perform the Funeral Prayer

1. Make the intention.

2. Raise your hands to the shoulders or to the ears, say *Allāhu Akbar* and fold your hands as you do in normal prayer.

3. Recite Surat *Al-Fātihah*.

4. **Say** *Allāhu Akbar* **again** and invoke the blessing of Allāh on the Prophet (peace and blessing of Allāh be upon him), by reading the same supplication which you read at the end of normal prayer.

5. **Say** *Alldhu Akbar* **third time** and read one or more of the following supplications:

(A)

اَللّٰهُمَّ اغْفِرْ لَهُ وَارْحَمْهُ وَعَافِهِ وَاعْفُ عَنْهُ وَاَكْرِمْ نُزْلَهُ وَ وَسِّعْ مُدْخَلَهُ وَ اغْسِلْهُ بِالْمَاءِ وَالثَّلْجِ وَالْبَرَدِ، وَنَقِّهِ مِنَ الْخَطَايَا كَمَا نَقَّيْتَ الثَّوْبَ الْاَبْيَضَ مِنَ الدَّنَسِ، وَاَبْدِلْهُ دَارًا خَيْرًا مِّنْ دَارِهِ وَاَهْلًا خَيْرًا مِّنْ اَهْلِهِ وَزَوْجًا خَيْرًا مِّنْ زَوْجِهِ وَ اَدْخِلْهُ الْجَنَّةَ وَاَعِذْهُ مِنْ عَذَابِ الْقَبْرِ وَعَذَابِ النَّارِ.

*Allaahummagh-fir lahu warhamhu wa 'aafihi wa'fu
'anhu wa akrim nuzulahu wa wassi 'mudkhalahu
waghsilhu bil-maa'i wath-thalji wal-barad. Wa naqqihi
minal-khataayaa kamaa naqqaytath-thawbal-abyada
minad-danas. Wa abdilhu daaran khayram-min daarihi
wa ahlan khayram-min ahlihi wa zawjan khayram-min
zawjihi wa adkhilul jannata wa a'idhhu min 'adhaabil-
qabri wa min 'adhaabin-Naar.*

(O Allāh, forgive him, have mercy on him, pardon him,
protect him, give him good hospitality, and widen his
abode. Cleanse him with water, snow and hail, and
purify him from sins as You purify white clothes from
dirt. And grant him abode better than his abode, a family
better than his family, a spouse better than his spouse
and admit him into Paradise and protect him from the
punishment of the grave and the punishment of the Fire.)
(Muslim)

(B)

اَللّٰهُمَّ اغْفِرْ لِحَيِّنَا وَمَيِّتِنَا وَشَاهِدِنَا وَغَآئِبِنَا وَ
صَغِيْرِنَا وَكَبِيْرِنَا وَذَكَرِنَا وَأُنْثَانَا، اَللّٰهُمَّ مَنْ أَحْيَيْتَهٗ
مِنَّا فَأَحْيِهٖ عَلَى الْإِسْلَامِ وَمَنْ تَوَفَّيْتَهٗ مِنَّا فَتَوَفَّهٗ عَلَى
الْإِيْمَانِ، اَللّٰهُمَّ لَا تَحْرِمْنَا أَجْرَهٗ وَلَا تُضِلَّنَا بَعْدَهٗ.

Allaahummagh-fir lihayyinaa wa mayyitinaa wa
shaahidinaa wa ghaa'ibinaa wa sagheerinaa wa
kabeerinaa wa dhakarinaa wa unthaanaa.
Allaahumma man ahyaytahu minnaa fa ahyihi 'alal-
Islaam, wa man tawaffaytahu minnaa fatawaffahu
'alal-Eemaan. Allaahumma laa tahrimnaa ajrahu wa
laa tudillanaa ba 'dahu.

(O Allāh, forgive our living and our dead, our present
and our absent, our young and our old, our male and our
female. O Allāh, the one of us You keep alive, keep him
alive on Islam, and the one of us whom You cause to
die, let him die in Faith. O Allāh, do not deprive us of the
reward for him, and do not make us go astray after him.)
(Ahmad, Abu Dāwud, At-Tirmidhi and Ibn Mājah)

If the deceased is a child then the following supplication should be said:

اَللَّهُمَّ اجْعَلْهُ لَنَا سَلَفًا وَفَرَطًا وَذُخْرًا وَاَجْرًا

Allaahummaj-'alhu lanaa salafan wa faratan wa dhukhran wa ajra.

(O Allāh, make him for us a forebear, an advance, a treasure and a reward.)

6. Say *Allāhu Akbar* fourth time and turn your face to the right saying;

اَلسَّلَامُ عَلَيْكُمْ وَرَحْمَةُ اللهِ

As-salaamu 'alaykum wa rahmatullaah
(Peace be on you and Allāh's mercy.)

Then to the left saying:

اَلسَّلَامُ عَلَيْكُمْ وَرَحْمَةُ اللهِ

As -salaamu 'alaykum wa rahmatullaah.
(Peace be on you and Allāh's mercy.)

Notes: